FloweTry

A Collection of 108 Poetic Flows on Life, Love, and Liturgical Issues

DR. TIFFANIE TATE MOORE

ISBN 978-1-63874-606-5 (paperback)
ISBN 978-1-63874-607-2 (digital)

Christian Faith Publishing, Inc.
832 Park Avenue
Meadville, PA 16335
www.christianfaithpublishing.com

Printed in the United States of America

To Nathaniel and Mia, you two mean the world to me.

I am thankful for the support of my family and friends during this process. Thank you, Arthur, for encouraging me to submit my poems to a publisher. Thank you, heavenly Father, for inspiring me to write.

I am thankful for the love of my mother, Aunderia, and my mom-tee Mae.

Contents

Life

Ode to Mom

Thank you, Lord, for the mother You gave.
She taught me how to behave.
She taught me to read your word.
Despite my circumstances, it is Your I will serve.

Thank you, Lord.
Thank you, Lord.
Thank you, Lord, for the mother you gave me.

She taught me to live for you,
And to give You praise, despite what I'm going through.
She taught me that Christians all fall,
But you, dear Lord, will see us through it all.

Thank you, Lord.
Thank you, Lord.
Thank you, Lord, for the mother You gave me.

She taught me to hide Your word in my heart,
And from Your presence, never to part.
She taught me to never let go of Your hand,
Your unchanging hand.
And, on the word of God, to always stand, stand,
Always stand.

She taught me how to call on Your name, in my time of need, and in
    my time of praise.
She taught me to have a reverent heart,

And with each new day, with prayer I should start.
Lord, I thank You
Lord, I thank You
Yes, I thank You for the mother you gave me.

Mom-tee

Born as your niece but raised as your daughter, you served in the role
   of both mother and father.
I am who I am because you loved me.
God blessed me with you, and I want the world to see.
You are the best ever mom-tee.

A mom-tee is a woman with the birthright of being my auntie.
She rose above her station to also serve as mother to me.
She was already raising her own children as a single mother.
I joined the ranks of her household, and she provides a love like no other.

Count yourself blessed if you have a mom-tee in your life.
Perhaps she was initially a sister, a friend, or even a neighbor's wife.
So we must remain very thankful for the love that a mom-tee gives.
We must pay it forward to help others thrive, survive, and live.

Dear Officer

Dear Officer, I know your job is hard.
I know you carry a gun and are always on guard.
Please, please hear my plea.
The color of my skin does not make me guilty, you see.
Please look beyond the color of my skin.
Look at the situation and take it all in.
I do not have a gun, and I am not a threat.
Please do not fire your gun and kill me just yet.

Dear Officer, I am a human being too.
I have family and friends just like you.
When you arrive and my hands are in the air,
Please find it in your heart my life to spare.
Even if I broke the law, the system should play out.
A jury should be the ones to determine guilt beyond reasonable doubt.

Dear Officer, please don't execute me.
I deserve to live too, you see.

A Letter to My Child

Mama, mama, is this how we make America great?
A nation overflowing with racial hate?
A nation reverting to the racist mentality of the past.
There is a dark shadow growing in our country, and I don't know how long it will last.

My child, my child, when you fail to learn from history, it is doomed to repeat itself, you see.
Ignorance alone is not a good justification because you see our people need a re-education if there is any desire to save this nation.
You must understand our country's history.
When the Constitution was written, Black people were not free.
We weren't even counted to be represented equally.

The US president quotes segregationists and invokes an 1807 Insurrection Act.
The America that he longs for is not great, and that is a fact.
A past history of racial oppression and overt bigotry.
This president does not represent the US, you see.

We have always struggled for equal protection under the law.
We evolved from slavery, but my feelings are still raw.
America has never dealt with the deep scars of its racist past.
The socioeconomic and political issues from it still last.

When slavery is brought up, the general thought is "get over it."
America memorializes the Jewish Holocaust but hides from its own shit.

We as a country are not where we need to be.
The land of the brave and home of the free does not always apply to you and to me.

The color of our black skin has been weaponized.
People judge us based on their eyes.
Seeing the content of my character is just a joke because half of America is not *woke*.
For far too long, America has hid from its oppressive past, but our country is bound by it like a porcelain cast.
We must remember and learn from former missteps and mistakes, that is truly the only way to be *great*.

Mama, mama, what can we do?
How can we change the system for me and you?
Speak up, speak out, and take time to *vote*.
We must challenge the system, maybe even revolt.

All change in America came from blood, sweat, and tears.
The abolition of slavery, the women's suffrage movement, the Civil Rights era evolved from protesters who moved past their fears.
They challenged the system, the status quo.
Our country has forgotten this, you know.

My child, my child, America has never embraced change easily.
It's always gone down kicking and screaming, you see.
No one really likes change because it's different from what they know.
But change is required if you want to grow.

Love always,
Mama

It's *the Law*

"It's the law" is just not enough.
Trying to swallow that pill is just too tough.
The initial laws of our land were very exclusive.
It took time and a demand for change to make them inclusive.

History proves "It's the law" is not a good justification for any poor
    action or deed as an explanation.
Laws have a history of being skewed, based on bias.
American laws were made by white males who were pious.
The law is often a reflection of the people.
Laws had to be changed to treat all as equal.

"It's the law" excluded women from having rights.
It took rebellious women to challenge that thinking, those who had
    a willingness to fight.
Women achieved the right to vote one hundred years ago, and it was
    a fight against the male ego.

"It's the law" once condoned slavery.
It took a civil war in which the north won bravely.
Jim Crow laws then ruled the land, and oppression of Black people
    was the plan.

"It's the law" allowed public lynching of Blacks.
The Ku Klux Klan legally organized attacks.
Segregation was the law, and integration was the flaw.

"It's the law" is limited because laws need change.
As we progress as a nation, a "more perfect union" comes within visible range.

"I was just following laws and orders," a failed Nuremberg defense.
For carelessly taking the life of another, there is no recompense.
Bad laws do not justify cruelty and abuse of one another.
We must change outdated laws and take responsibility for our brother.

Laws change, and so do people.
We must learn to treat everyone as equal.
Law and order are nice sentiments, but without love and compassion, they set a poor precedent.

My Country / Of Thee I Sing

My country, 'tis of thee,
Sweet land of liberty,
But wait, that doesn't really apply to me. Nevertheless, of thee I sing.

Land where my fathers died.
From every mountainside, let freedom ring!
But wait, except for the Black community,
In that group, this will not apply to thee.
Nevertheless, of thee I sing.

So what exactly does it mean to be free?
Freedom is the right to act, speak, or think without hindrance, you
    see.
That surely does not apply to me.
Nevertheless, of thee I sing.

From slavery till this present day,
America still has not found a way,
To let "all lives" have a say.
Nevertheless, of thee I sing.

Native Americans were slaughtered for this land,
Black slaves built this country and its wealth by hand,
But our exclusion was the master plan.
Nevertheless, of thee I sing.

The Constitution's Three-Fifths Compromise,
It still brings tears to my eyes.

The fugitive slave clause
put the idea of freedom on pause.
Nevertheless, of thee I sing.

In 1896, Plessy v. Ferguson,
"Separate but equal" won.
This has never truly been undone.
Nevertheless, of thee I sing.

The white-black wealth, health, and economic disparity,
It should be a wake-up call for you and me.
True, equality is what is needed, you see,
So we must change our song.

We must change our song
We must change our song

God bless America, land that I love.
Stand beside her and guide her
Through the night with the light from above.
Let her fight against all racial disparities,
Against the hatemongers please!
Yes! Of thee I joyfully sing.

This is how we make and keep America great.
By the abolishment of racial hate, that's how we make America great.
Let us band together for those in need.
This is how we help America succeed.
Yes! Of thee I joyfully sing.
From the mountains to the prairies,
To the oceans white with foam,
God bless America, my home sweet home.
God bless America, my home sweet home.

Your Rights

The First Amendment of the Constitution allows freedom of speech.
Good or bad, right or wrong, it's up to us to teach.
Only America wants to glorify those who lost. There are no statues of
    Adolf Hitler for his role in the Jewish Holocaust.

Americans have a right to hate.
It doesn't matter that that is not how you make America great.
President Trump's supporters will continue to support him no matter
    what you say.
Say a prayer, take a deep breath, and go about your day.

Our great nation is at a pivotal point.
With Trump's biased views, he can only disappoint.
Nothing for Black people has ever come easily.
We have always had to fight in order to just "be."

After slavery was abolished, no one was free.
"Separate and unequal" was the policy.
From slavery to Jim Crow to the Civil Rights fight, we have had to
    be strong, we have had to unite.

This revolution of policing is long overdue.
We must continue to demand justice and a system that is fair and true.
We must *vote* for the America of tomorrow,
one without racial disparity.
A nation that will be a beacon of light for the rest of the world to see.

History will judge Trump supporters and his alternative facts.
All we can do is be true to ourselves and try to relax.
Freedom of speech applies to everyone, even if we disagree when all
is said and done.

So let the racists be racist. That is what they do.
I pray to God they don't create policy for me and you.
So just thank them for letting their true colors show, so try not to be
bothered with them because now you know.

Sticks and Stones

Sticks and stones may break my bones, but bones mend.
Hateful words can pierce a soul, and the damage may never end.
The stain of slavery still casts a shadow in all aspects of American life.
Black people are expected to "get over" slavery without any strife.
People of color have been relegated to urban hoods and underfunded
    schools.
When we question the status quo, we are called entitled fools.
We have drifted from a society of "we" to one of "me."
Let us try to get back to "we the people" as we try to have everyone
    treated equal.

The Skin You Are In

It is amazing how some people treat others differently based on the
color of the skin they are in.
It is funny because no one picked the race they were born within.
We do not choose our parents or the land we call home.
No person is "pure" anything if we took a look at their chromosomes.
No one selects their genetics, and that is a matter of fact.
Why can't everyone be treated equal? Can we make that pact?

The Thirteenth Amendment of the Constitution abolished slavery
and involuntary servitude, except for the punishment of a crime.
Mass incarceration of Blacks in our nation is the new form of slavery
in our time.

Dr. King was arrested about thirty times or so.
During his time, America hated him, or did you not know?
The FBI spied on King and viewed his rhetoric as "extreme."
As he challenged the status quo, he was not held in esteem.
I am amazed that after his assassination, they could not find who did
it in this great nation.

A nation divided will eventually fail, and bigoted thinking will drive
our nation straight to hell.
Do not think of yourself as being better than those with darker skin.
Our country can only get better when we treat everyone as equal
despite the color of the skin they are in.

Better

Is it better yet?
Do you have regret?
Just keep pressing forward and through the tough road ahead of you.
Sometimes it is better to see things in the rear view,
Out of fear of things that are straight ahead in front of you.
Do not be afraid of what is to come.
Only you really know where you are actually coming from.
When departing a bad situation, anything better is a welcome
    invitation.
Better is on the way. Push aside any thoughts of dismay.
Yes, it will get better.

Bless the Children

Bless the children.
Keep them as they come and go.
Bless the children.
Lord, let them feel Your presence and know
That you are with them, and you'll never leave their side.
All they must do, is stay in Your word and let You be their guide.
Bless the children.
Lord, please bless the children.

Why

Why me?
Why must I hurt?
Why must I feel pain?
Why must I endure sorrow?
Why must I withstand the rain?

Hope

People often ask, What is wrong with me?
How can I smile living in my circumstances that they see?
But I've got faith, greater than a mustard seed.
My faith and hope in Christ helps me to live free.

Behind My Smile

Behind my smile, I suffer in silence, for only You know what I'm really going through.

Behind my smile, the fake jokes, and laughter, You see the heartache and the tears that fall.

You see the pain.

You see the mental anguish and strain.

You see the truth behind my smile.

Mother, Don't You Know

Mother, don't you know, that I miss you?
Mother, don't you know, a part of me died with you?
Mother, don't you know, you will live forever in my heart?
Mother, don't you know, from my heart you will never depart?
Mother, don't you know, mother don't you know?

Our life together, was far from perfect,
But you loved me.
But you loved me.

We had some bumps in this thing called life,
Episodes of resentment, and strife.
Through it all, you were always there.
I reflect back on our memories, and I know that you cared.

For your imperfect times, I forgive you.
For my obnoxious times, I hope that you forgive me too.
Mother, don't you know, that I miss you?
Mother, don't you know, a part of me died with you?
Mother, don't you know, you will live forever in my heart?
Mother, don't you know, from my heart you will never depart?
Mother, don't you know, mother, don't you know?

Move

Because you cannot afford not to.
Move.
Because your heart is depending on you.
Move.
Because it is what your body needs you to do.
Move.

Once you start to move, just keep moving.
Walk, run, swim, jog, or dance.
Do whatever you must do to give good health a chance.
Just move.

Heaven's Party

There's a party going on in heaven, a celebration like none before.
Family and friends who have predeceased us are dancing on heaven's floor
As they celebrate gaining another angel.
Oh, what I would give to peek through that door.

Those of us left behind on earth are filled with grief, and our hearts are heavy.
We mourn for those who are gone, and our sorrow is about to break the levy.
Tears are about to fall like rain.
Only sweet memories of you and God's grace can ease the pain.

Hood

You can take the girl out of the hood, but you can't take the hood
   out of the girl.
She has a heart of gold, but she has been hardened by this world.
Yes, she is sweet and sassy.
She can dress to the nines and is very classy.
No, don't slip up and rub her the wrong way.
She can read, write, and dress you down before sending you on your
   way.

Being from the hood, it is generally understood that to achieve our
   dreams, we must be better than good.
As around-the-way girls, we know we must be the best to conquer
   this world.
The neighborhood molds us to be our best as long as we use our
   energy to rise above the rest.
Hats off to all my fellow peeps from the hood. Show where you came
   from with pride because it's all good.

The Reckoning

That great day of reckoning is now drawing near.
The racists in our society are trying to fan the flames of fear.
Fear that the status quo is crumbling and will fall,
As we as a nation demand equal justice for all.

The reckoning of America's sordid history due to its deeds of the
    past.
The lasting effects of those deeds are being discussed at last.
Native Americans were killed for this land we call home.
Now they are confined to reservations that limit where they roam.

The reckoning that our great nation was born in 1776.
But there was an evil looming that the Constitution did not fix.
Laws were made to preserve the freedom of everyone except the slave.
Millions of slaves were beaten and slaughtered because they would
    not conform or "behave."

The reckoning of the historic divide between the Confederate South
    and Union North.
There has been a movement to glorify slavery from that point forth.
The Civil War was fought, and the Union North won.
So why are statues erected in memory of those southern treasonous
    sons of guns?

You did not need to own slaves to reap the benefit.
Recognizing white privilege would be a good start of beneficence.
And to say that something matters means it has importance or
    significance.

Life, It Will Get Better

Life, it will get better, if you give it time.
Troubles don't last forever. Just hang in there, for tomorrow the sun
  will shine.

The storms of life will surely come.
And no, they are not fun.
Sometimes they make you feel so low.
You may think there is nowhere else to go.
The storms are there to help you grow.
Jesus is with you, so please know

Life, it will get better, if you give it time.
Troubles don't last forever. Just hang in there, for tomorrow the sun
  will shine.

Your testimony will come from your test.
Be patient and trust in God.
He can handle the rest.
We already have the victory.
God wants us to rely on Him so we can see.

Life, it will get better, if you give it time.
Troubles won't last forever. Just hang in there, for tomorrow the sun
  will shine.

Dear White People

Dear white people, we can all get along.
Please do not stick your head in the sand and pretend like nothing is wrong.
I know you did not cause the problem, but you can help fix it.
Racism is an issue that can only be addressed if you admit it.
Please do not pretend no race problem exists.
Let us pull together and not let the frustration of people of color be dismissed.

All Lives v. Black Lives

When I think about my Christian religion, my soul begins to shake, because unfortunately, some of my fellow followers of Christ are just not awake.
When I say Black lives matter, they reflectively say, "All lives do."
I do not contest that point, and I believe that it is true too.
But at the present time, Black lives are excluded. We wouldn't have to say that Black lives matter if they were already included.

Trumpers, Trumpers

Trumpers, Trumpers, do what you do.
Forever stand by him and disbelieve what is true.
No one can speak ill of your favorite president.
The truth does not matter. Just follow Trump's Twitter vent.

Trumpers, Trumpers, stand tall by his side,
For Trump can absolutely do no wrong in your eyes.
Even if the words out of his mouth are lies, lies, and lies.

Trumpers, Trumpers, cast your morals away
As you overlook how he treats his fellow man from day to day.
What he does is surely not what Jesus would do.
No worries, I'm still your friend. I won't judge you.

Trumpers, Trumpers, is he really worth the cost?
The stock market is up, but the soul of our country is being lost.
Should you be called a racist just because you voted for one?
Not by me, but history will decide when all is said and done.

Trumpers, Trumpers, come to his defense every chance you get.
When history judges you, then there might be some regret.

Father, Forgive Us

Dear heavenly Father, please forgive us,
For we know exactly what we do
As we have strayed far away from you.

We have become a society all about "me."
We neglect each other and forsake the "we."
We no longer value people but mainly money.
Oh Father, please forgive us

Father, forgive us.
We have abandoned the pursuit of justice.
People of color are imprisoned at an astronomical rate.
We are failing to address racial profiling based on underlying hate.

Father, forgive us.
Speaking out against police brutality has turned into a debate over
    monuments and flags instead of the violence we see.
We took prayer out of schools but kept Your name on our money.
Our priorities are mixed up, and this is not funny.

We won't wear masks to prevent the spread of COVID-19.
We put the lives of our fellow man in jeopardy, which is mean.
Losing loved ones always causes heartache and pain.
The COVID-19 loss of lives our country is suffering makes tears fall
    from my eyes like rain.
Father, forgive us.

Baby Grown Up

My baby is all grown up
I'm happy, but I cry
I'm not ready to let go
But I know that it's your time to fly

So it's okay for you to go
Go spread your wings and learn to fly
Go find your way in this crazy world

Hypocrisy

We all live lives of hypocrisy.
If this doesn't apply to you, please disregard me.

Can you see it? The hypocrisy.
Does it apply to both of us, you, or me?
Some refuse to wear a mask for protection from COVID-19.
They say masks infringe on their rights, and some have been down-
    right mean.
They scream, shout, and destroy store mask displays in protest.
They call Black Lives Matter marchers criminals and thugs for their
    nonviolent unrest.

Can you see it? The hypocrisy.
Does it apply to both of us, you, or me?
When opposition questions Trump's behavior, "Thou shall not
    judge" is what Trump followers say.
They defend his unloving, cruel, and bigot behavior as they turn
    their head and look away.

Can you see it? The hypocrisy.
Does it apply to both of us, you or me?
"All lives matter" but only to a certain extent.
Some are just *pro-birth* and not *pro-life* so please give me a moment
    to just *vent*:
Reverse the Affordable Care Act?
No affordable medical care, no coverage for preexisting conditions,
    and no contraception?
Reverse Roe v. Wade, a case that years ago was won?

Have women revert to self-abortions, coat hangers, and throwing themselves down stairs?

It matters not that God gives us free will because some in our population just don't care.

Can you see it? The hypocrisy.

Does it apply to both of us, you, or me?

The minority of America wants to impose their views on the majority.

Stealing the Supreme Court seat before the election is just a sad sight to see.

Congressional republicans stole the seat from President Obama when he had a year left in his term.

Now with three months left in Trump's term, they are trying to push through a candidate that I pray they cannot confirm.

If republicans and Trump win their upcoming election, they should fill the seat.

If Trump fails to win, then Biden can fill it after Trump's defeat.

That Is Not Okay

Can I go to Taco Bell for lunch?
Sure, I can.
While there can I order a Big Mac?
I can ask, but they can't provide it.
That is not okay.

Can I send a pregnant woman who is ten weeks pregnant to labor
    and delivery?
Sure, I can.
While there can I ask the L&D nurses to apply fetal monitoring?
I can ask, but they can't provide it.
That is not okay.

Can I go to the dentist for teeth cleaning while experiencing pelvic
    pain?
Sure, I can.
While there can I ask for a pelvic ultrasound?
I can ask, but they can't provide it.
That is not okay.

Police officers are there to protect and serve.
To uphold the law.
So *why* is it reasonable to expect the police to function in a variety of
    functions that they are not trained to deal with?
That is not okay.
Defund the police is *not* abolish the police.

The demands that we place on the police are unreasonable. Their
   sole function should be to *protect*, *serve*, and *uphold* the law, and
   we as a nation should designate other agencies to do the rest.
This is okay.

Agree to Disagree

Let us agree to disagree.
How Trump still has followers baffles me.
They turn a blind eye to his bullying and cruelty.
America is the great butt of all jokes, but they just can't see.
So let us just agree to disagree.

Disagreeing political views were okay in the past.
We laughed at each other, and political anger did not last.
Now extremists want to kidnap governors as we drift toward anarchy.
No condemnation from our president as he spews words to reinforce
    the patriarchy.
So let us just agree to disagree.

Taxes

No one loves taxes, but they must be paid.
That financial support keeps our country's finances made in the
shade.
Tax revenue pays our police, firemen, and teachers, just to name a
few.
How can you love America when you fail to render what is finan-
cially due?

America is financed by taxes, and all must pay their part.
"The more you make the more Uncle Sam takes" has been the game
from the start.
Jesus was a revolutionary and *not* a people pleaser.
When asked about taxes, even Jesus said, "Render unto Caesar what
is Caesar's."

Yes, the tax game is lame, and nobody really wants to give their hard-
earned money away.
Our country must be financed, and taxes are the price we pay.
Third world countries desire what we have, and what we have is not
free.
Millionaires and billionaires in our country should pay their fair
share in taxes or flee.

Our current president gives more in taxes to other countries than the
    one he currently runs.
That is not smart, it's a travesty, and something must be done.
Our tax code needs an overhaul to modify loopholes used by the rich.
Come November we must *unite* and vote out that son of a b###h!

Taxes support our military too.
If you don't want to pay taxes, there is still something you can do.
Please join our military. Uncle Sam wants you.

Life Goes On

So your candidate didn't win the election.
Please know that it's okay.
God is still the same God of yesterday and today.
Yes, in 2016 God permitted Trump to win,
And He is the one who prevented it from happening in 2020 again.

Everyone has been there at some point in time.
Yes, Trump lost, so out of your self-pity you must climb.
We are Americans, and no one person makes us great.
We are a melting pot of people and must stray from racial hate.
Life goes on.
We must turn the page to see our new dawn.
Out of the ashes of an attempted coup we must rise.
We are a shining beacon of democracy in the world's eyes.

Let us take our place on the world stage.
Let us not put immigrant children in a cage.
Life goes on. Yes, this is true.
History has its eyes on me and you.

Happy Black History Month

Why celebrate Black history?
Because the history of Blacks in America remains a mystery.
Contributions by Blacks to America are only known by few.
This history is excluded from primary education. It's sad but true.

Let us usher in these twenty-eight days with an open mind.
Please be patient with those who don't know anything and treat them
    kind.
Daily please share a Black history fact.
Do it with a smile and the best tact.

Ambitious Dreamer

Be an ambitious dreamer.
Do not limit yourself.
When you envision your future, seek happiness over wealth.
Do not let other people step on your dreams.
Do not let them force you into a reality of "seems."
Of what "seems" to be what is best for you.
Trust yourself. You know what you want to do.

The Other Side

The other side is often out of view,
Especially when there is huge mountain before you.
Just take it day by day and one step at a time.
When you get past, this life will be sublime.

Life can be hard from time to time.
Sometimes you can be so broke you ain't even got a dime.
If you keep moving, this phase will be temporary.
Push toward your goals and in self-pity, do not tarry.

Keep climbing the mountain even if you must slow your stride.
Once you get to the top, the view alone will fill you with self-pride.
If you give up and quit moving, you will never reach the other side.

Alternative Facts

The term *alternative fact* was coined by the Trump administration.
What is an alternative fact? Well, it is called a lie in any other nation.
It is when you take the truth and distort it to fit your narrative.
It is the exact opposite of the truth and the reality in which you live.

America Amiss

The USA is the greatest country in history.
I know that I am biased, for it is my homeland, the land of the brave
and free.
It has served as a beacon of hope for all the world to see.
Unfortunately, that light has been tarnished by racial hate and bigotry.
America has gone amiss, and we must set things right.
We must get back to our fundamentals and hold up the light.

"Give me your tired, your poor,…masses" written on the Statue of
Liberty.
We are an immigrant nation making it difficult for immigrant entry.
Canadians are free to come and go with minimal difficulty.
Southern neighbors have to jump through hoops and, from border
patrol, flee.
Is there something ominous at play here? I do not know.
I do not want to believe it pertains to the amount of pigmented skin
they show.

America has gone amiss, but we can get back on track.
We need to come together, help our fellow man, and pick up the
slack.
When we work together as a nation, we can do anything.
Welcoming immigrants in orderly is the best way to let freedom ring.

Abuse

Verbal and emotional abuse are still abuse.
It is not okay just because it is not predicated with alcohol and drug use.
For years I suffered with that neck noose.
This is the year that I break loose.

So I am supposed to be grateful that you did not physically hit me?
Yes, there were no scars for all the world to see.
Unfortunately, you bruised our children and I internally.
Only time will heal my pain when I am free.

Community

Growing up in the inner city, there was an atmosphere of community.
We played in the streets with neighboring kids and looked out for
the collective we.
We didn't view ourselves as poor because we were all in the same
boat.
We were all latchkey kids who bought cigarettes from the corner
store with a note.

Community kids took care of each other.
We looked out for ourselves like a brother.
When all of us kids arrived at our empty houses after school, we all
wanted a snack.
I made sugar and syrup sandwiches for the kids on my street and
took them out to distribute and unpack.
After gobbling up our unhealthy treat, we would play until the lights
came on in the street.
We parted and retired to our homes without missing a beat and
planned to do it again the next day when we would meet.

Family

Family are the people with whom your life you share.
They love and support you and are always there.
They are people on whom you can depend on and lean.
They love you even when you are obnoxious and obscene.

Family is more than the people to whom you are related.
It can include friends you have absorbed who keeps your spirits
    elated.
Friends who are now ad hoc sisters, brothers, or mothers.
When friends transition to family, there is a love shared like no other.

Whether you are family bound by blood or love, I am thankful you
    are in my life and sent from heaven above.

Love

Love?

How can you say that you love your fellow man when you won't take the time to lend a helping hand?

A hand to help people out of poverty. For one of the richest nations in the world, it's a travesty.

The mighty dollar says "In God We Trust," yet we abandoned the Word of God for worldly lust.

Longing for riches, power, and fame, it's just a distraction, so don't fall victim to the game.

If we focus on God and His will, everything will be all right if we just keep still.

Love, Bah Humbug

I love love, but it does not love me.
Just when I thought I found it, it eluded me.
Is love just an illusion that no one can see?
Chasing it around here and there, it must have been hiding under a rug.
I'm at the point when I think, Love, bah humbug.

Perhaps love is just not in my cards.
I'm weary of those who say they love me and come sniffing around my yard.
I'm afraid of a broken heart, so I stay on guard.
Experiencing a broken heart feels like being pierced with a glass shard.
I'm at the point when I think, Love, bah humbug.

Too for You

I'm just "too" for you.
Too dark skinned, you prefer a lighter tone.
It's okay that my color isn't in your zone.

I'm just "too" for you.
Too tall, as you prefer the vertically challenged.
A woman of my height is not easily managed.

I'm just "too" for you.
Too fat and unappealing for your taste.
I'm confident in my beauty, but with you it goes to waste.

I'm just "too" for you.
Too giving because you viewed our relationship as transactional.
Being called "your John" hurt and was just detestable.

I'm just "too" for you.
Too financially successful, a threat to your manhood.
As a couple, we would have been a team if only you understood.

I'm "too" for you.
Too rich because you say I'm trying to buy your love.
My generous spirit is nothing more than a blessing from above.

I'm just "too" for you.
Our relationship was one you could not see through.
I get it. I'm not your type.
I'm more your homie. Maybe you will pick me when I'm ripe.

I'm just "too" for you.
I'm too in love with you.
One person cannot provide enough love for two.

I'm just "too" for you.
Too much for you to handle at this time.
While there is no "we," I hope you enjoy this rhyme.

So into You

I'm so into you, what am I going to do
My heart belongs to you
My heart belongs to you
You don't feel the same, you think love is a game
And that is just a shame, but I'm still into you

My love is here
Waiting for you
And it's true
I'm so into you
I'm so into you

My love for you is real, I hope one day you'll feel
Feel the same about me
You took advantage of my love, I've chosen to rise above
Above the heartache and pain you've caused me

My love is here
Waiting for you
And it's true
I'm so into you
I'm so into you

You like to use and abuse me, so I must leave for the sake of me
I'll love you from afar
You don't love me back, and that is just a fact
You will always hold a piece of my heart

My love is here
Waiting for you
And it's true
I'm so into you
I'm so into you

If you have a change of heart, I'll be back in your arms and never depart
You can always count on me, from now to eternity

My love is here
Waiting for you
And it's true
I'm so into you
I'm so into you

Fairytale Love

Once upon a time, I dreamt of love.
You know, the type that fairytale stories are made of.
I dreamt of all the warm feelings encompassed thereof.
The love you think of when you see two turtledoves.

Fairytale love has its own attractive bling.
When in fairytale love, you hear the birds around you sing.
Watch out if you both have been hit by Cupid's arrow zing.
When two people are in love, it can lead to a wedding ring.

Fairytale loves makes you feel warm and fuzzy inside.
You can try to run from it, but you just can't hide.
Lean into it, buckle up, and get ready for the love roller-coaster ride.
You will find life fulfilling if in love you abide.

Love Song

You, you are my love song
You play on my mind all day long
You have my heart spinning around
You lift up my spirit when I'm down

You, you are my love song
Any time away from you just feels wrong
My love for you is true, and to you I belong
No one else can ever take your place
I can't imagine anyone ever matching your embrace

You, you are my love song
You, you are my love song

Friend

So you say that you want to be my friend.
So why did you have to wait for our marriage to end?
You tolerated me while we were married.
All the family obligations I alone carried.

Our marriage was supposed to be a partnership.
So let me fill you in on this little tip.
I forgive you for abandoning me.
For not being supportive emotionally.

You and I both know you did not give your best.
I'm enjoying my time alone and the much-needed rest.
I know I was not the perfect wife.
You could always count on me despite our strife.

Touch Me

A relationship with me is what you want.
I must be more than a woman on your arm for you to flaunt.
Touch me.
Tease me.
But when it comes down to it, you better please me.
You need to touch my heart.
You need to touch my mind.
Physical pleasure is nice, but that's just a small part of our time.

Touch my soul.
Help me feel whole.
Let us spend quality time together.
Touching me within will strengthen our relationship to withstand
  stormy weather.

I Go On

I go on
With you in my heart.
I go on
Even though we are apart.
I go on, I go on, I go on.

I go on
Despite not hearing the sound of your voice.
I go on.
I would have you here next to me if I had the choice.
I go on, I go on, I go on.

All

Give me all you've got, even if it's not a lot.
I'll give you all I can, and be your number one fan.
Always side by side, we can help each other's stride.
All of our brokenness can be mended with our love.
All my love I willingly give to you.
All of me for all of you.

God Loves You More

As much as I love you
More than words can express
My love can pass any test
But God loves you more

As much as I love you
More than actions can show
You need to know
That God loves you more

God loves you more
Your soul He adores
Your sin He forgives
In you He lives

Open up your heart
He'll give you a brand new start
Regardless of your sin
He helps you begin again.

There Is Nothing

There is nothing that you can do,
To stop Momma from loving you.
There is nothing that you can say,
To make Momma turn away.
Well, it's the same with Jesus,
He even goes a step above.
He sacrificed His life,
And showed a wretch like you and me love.
So no matter where you are,
No matter what you've been through.
Jesus is there, and He will take care of you.

There is nothing that you can do,
To stop Jesus from loving you.
There is nothing that you can say,
To make Jesus turn away.

You can be the chief of sin,
He will forgive and let you start again.
There is nothing that you can do,
To stop Jesus from loving you.

When You Love

When you love someone
What do you do to show you them care?

When you love someone
How do you show them you will always be there?

When you love someone
What do you do?

What do you do for Jesus
To thank Him for saving you?
What do you do for Jesus
To show that you love Him too!

When you love someone
What do you do?

What do you do for Jesus?
What do you do for Jesus?
What do you do for Jesus?

What do you do for Jesus
After He wraps His arms around you?
What do you do for Jesus
To show Him that your love is true?

Love

There is nothing that you can do
To ever make me stop loving you.
There is nothing that you can say
To ever drive me away.

My love is forever
Forever I will love you.
My love is forever
Forever I will love you.

WWJD?

What would Jesus do?
Would He be ashamed or proud of me and you?
Our world has strayed far from His word and will.
It took a pandemic for us to be still.
We must be still and know that God is still in control.

What would Jesus do?
Would He lock kids in cages separate from their family?
Would He deport "illegal" immigrants for all the world to see?
We were charged to love one another as Christ loved the church.
America, a nation built on immigration, has been knocked off of its
    high perch.

What would Jesus do?
Would He value money more than people?
Would He fight for the right for all to be treated fair and equal?
COVID-19 highlights the health racial disparity. Black and brown
    folks die at the highest rates, you see.
There is limited or no health care for people of color.
America, my rich nation, it's time to take responsibility for the care
    of your brother.

What would Jesus do?
Would He speak out for the downtrodden and the poor?
The Beatitudes of Christ demonstrate that, for sure.
When will we stop and be more like Christ?
When will we stop silently condoning racism and do what is right?

What would Jesus do?
At this moment in time, I doubt He's proud of me or you.
Climate change is destroying our earth.
The economy is valued more than a life is worth.
We must stop and do an about-face if we want to salvage salvation
    for the human race.

What would Jesus do?
Forgive us and shower mercy and grace over me and you.
Give us multiple opportunities to make this world a better place.
We must rise to the occasion so we can hear "well done" when we see
    Him face to face.

Never

I never thought that I would be where I am today.
When I said "I do," I believed that forever with him I would stay.
But things don't always go as we have planned.
It's time for me to value myself and to take a stand.

I never, no, never, I never planned on divorce.
Love is supposed to be easy, not something that you must force.
Perhaps we waited too long to go down this road.
I pray that we can at least be friends, for who knows what the future
    may hold?

I never believed that one day we would not be together.
I never believed our marriage we would sever.
Both of us, our vows we violated.
Both of us, with each other we are frustrated.

Resentment

I'm sorry I resent you, but I do.
The following are the reasons that I feel this way toward you.
Some things are big and others small. I doubt I can recount them all.

I feel as if I'm nothing more than your secretary.
When you need me, I am there, but when I need you, sometimes you
    don't really care.
I have often felt, in this relationship, alone because you seemed to be
    distant and in your own zone.

I've shouldered the brunt of everything since we've been together.
I'm tired and fed up and doubt things will ever get better.
I feel as if I'm nothing more than your bill fairy. I feel as if you
    couldn't care less about the burdens that I carry.

Having me tell our children and my aunt about my affair was petty
    of you and showed how little you cared.
You forever changed my relationship with our kids, and yet you seem
    clueless about what you did.
You never showed them what forgiveness looked like. You were con-
    stantly angry, and that just wasn't right.

You treated me poorly for the next three years. Your emotional abuse
    caused me much anguish, depression, and tears.
As I struggled to forgive me, you constantly pulled me down, and
    managed to turn my smile into a frown.

You were repeatedly distant and absent from our kids' events.
You would be asleep at home and missed many moments.
You can miss me with your attempt to now be father of the year.
Our kids are now grown, and I'm ready to change gears.

You are still holding on to anger against me and my family.
You are again absent from events, and everyone can see.
I am glad that you are now making friends and coming into your
    own because I would never want to leave you alone.

This decade of my life will be different than the past.
I will not live under guilty oppression. I will be free at last.
I don't mean to paint you as a villain, but unfortunately, in my life,
    that is the role you have been fillin'.

All of these words just to say, With you I don't think I can stay.
You will always have a special place in my heart, but now I believe it's
    time for me to depart.

I Don't

Once, I said "I do."
Now I say "I don't."
I will not be your doormat. No, sir, I won't.
Marriage is said to be an institution.
Mine was a looney bin.
It was also like a prison cell in which I died daily within.

Love You

I love you, and I thought that you should know
I'll stay by your side and never let you go.
My goal is to bring you happiness.
Let me help alleviate your stress.

I love you and want to stay by your side.
Let's stay together forever and let love be our guide.
If at any time you no longer want to be with me,
Please let me know so we can redefine "we."

I love you, and we can just be friends if you want to.
Wanting you in my life forever still remains true.
Hearing your voice fills me with love and relief.
How I love you so much brings me disbelief.

I love you and long to be in your arms.
I can't withstand your smile and southern charms.
I'm vulnerable with you, and my defenses you disarm.
I am 100 percent yours, so don't let it bring you alarm.

I love you, please know that my love is true.
Nothing you can do will make me stop loving you.
If you decide you no longer want me,
I love you enough to set you free.

Kindness or Weakness

Please do not take my kindness for weakness because that is just not
   cool.
Despite what you may think, I will not play your little fool.
I have a wealth of sentiments in my emotional pool.
If you're lucky to receive my love, then you have found a jewel.
My kindness is not a weakness for you to abuse as a tool.

Like Beyoncé, I can upgrade you because I'm just that kind.
Sit back, relax. You ain't seen nothin' yet, because baby, I will blow
   your mind.
No matter how hard you look, another woman like me you will
   never find.

Yes, I exude kindness, but that does not make me weak.
I am tough, but when my heart is broken, my eyes will leak.
In the midst of my tears, I am not meek.
Abuse my kindness, and you and I will be through.
Despite what you think of me, I am strong enough to leave you.

Hearts

I do not care that we were born ages apart.
Does age really matter when we see each other heart-to-heart?
When we met, there was something special about you. I could feel it
    from the start.
I never dreamed I would want to be with you forever and never part.

I blew the feeling off and thought, Where did that come from? It felt
    strange.
The moment our hearts connected, that is when my world changed.
From that moment forward I was drawn to you.
You can always call on me because for you there is nothing I would
    not do.

Please believe me when I say that my heart is yours.
Our hearts connect on another level, and it is you that I adore.
So, my dear, please do not worry when others try to break us apart.
We can conquer anything together as long as we remain heart-to-heart.

The Institution

The institution of marriage can range from bliss to misery.
Where it falls on the spectrum of happiness is for you to see.
Just as love and happiness can morph into rage and despair.
The institution of marriage can become devoid of love and care.

An institution can be a custom or a gathering place.
Marriage is an institution that people often run into without haste.
Prison is an institution that, if you spend your life in it, is a waste.
Insane asylums are institutions people try to avoid and never face.
Only you can understand the challenges in your life's race.

What do you do when your marriage becomes a prison and institution of insanity?
The longer you stay in it, you lose your humanity.
The longer you stay, your language increases in profanity.
Are you staying for the optics or out of pure vanity?
There is no love there. That has been cut off like a double amputee.
Life is just going through the motions and is pure mundanity.

One hundred percent of divorces begin with the institution of marriage.
Despite my sarcasm, I believe in love, and it I will not disparage.
My goal is to inform you of potential pitfalls ahead.
So please be fully aware of with whom you decide to share your bed.
Please be very conscious of with whom you share your life.
Can we make a life together? Do I want to be their wife?
Do I want to be institutionalized with them for the rest of my life?

We

We consists of you and me
I want us to be together throughout eternity
I refuse to let others disrupt our happiness
People will try to break us up, but we will not stress
We are strong enough to withstand any test

We can do anything we put our hearts and minds to
If we put our pride aside, there is nothing we can't talk our way through
Our future together is very bright
God is love, and He is our guiding light
We must stay in love to keep everything right

We are strong and with each other belong
When we are apart from each other, we long
We must let out love grow and continue to take flight
We must fight to keep our love tight
We must stay together and never stray
We must not let people get in our way

Love Love

I love love and the idea thereof
Cupid's arrow must have given me a shove
Into a love unanticipated
I'm glad to experience this love long-awaited

I love love and the joy I feel
Spending time with him seems so surreal
I never thought that I'd be in this place
I'm so excited just to see his face

I love love and my happiness inside
I am excited to take this ride
His love provides me an emotional high
I don't want our love to ever die

I love love and don't want it to end
If he breaks my heart, it might not mend
Despite the risk, my love I freely give
May our love for each other forever live.

Love Spectrum

I love you, just not as much as I use to.
I love you, just not enough to do that for you.
I love you, but I love that person more than you.
Where on the love spectrum do you fall onto?

Oh, yes, the love spectrum is totally real.
Women and men can tip toe around it, but eventually they will have
    to deal with reality and pay the bill.
All love is not equal so don't you dare try to say so.
Recall all of your ex lovers and in your heart you will know.

Hidden Tears

I can't count how many nights I cried myself to sleep.
I hid my face in my pillow and cried silently as to not make a peep.
I often cried in the shower so my tears would not show.
I kept my tears hidden because I did not want to let anyone know.

Happiness is an inside job.
What do you do when all you want to do is sob?
You feel like a failure for the inability to fix yourself and your feelings.
You go round and round in your mind with unrealistic dealings.
You slip into a deeper depression well.
Life begins to feel like a living hell.

Hidden tears become harder to hide.
You don't want to share your depression with friends due to pride.
You pray for God to take the emotional pain away.
You lay in bed, and the hidden tears begin to fall again from day to
    day on instant replay.

You Can't

You can't love me the way that I need you to.
Don't worry, it's okay. I am not mad at you.
We once had a love that was really true.
I now realize that what we once shared is completely through.

You can't give yourself to me as I am not your priority.
I refuse to sit back and wishfully wait and see.
We both deserve a love that empowers us and sets us both free.
No worries, I'm your friend now and throughout eternity.

You can't love me because you like me more.
I think it's sweet that I'm someone you adore.
Adoration is not enough to open love's door.
An intimate relationship requires so much more.

You can't love me because I'm not "the one."
Despite trying to rekindle what we had, it is obvious that our love is
    done.
At least we can say that during our limited time together, we had fun.
I wish you the best in your next love run.

Not So Much

I wanted you to be my end game, but as it turns out, not so much.
I wanted you to be the last man that I would ever touch.
I wanted you to be the man with whom I would say "I do."
That will not so much be a reality for us two.

You say you love me, but your actions don't always show it.
You fail to display your love. You just seem to blow it.
A man makes a way, not an excuse.
I want a real relationship, not an elaborate ruse.
Our destinies are no longer intermingled, and I hope you enjoy being
    single.

Back

How did we get back here?
How did we get back to this place?
I've longed to be back here.
Oh, how I have missed your sweet embrace.

Oh, to be back in each other's arms.
You are setting off all my alarms.
Should I run away or just fall in?
Do I head back down this road again?
You once broke my heart.
Should I stop it before it starts?
But this love it feels so good.
I just don't know if I really should.

To have you back is a miracle.
I choose to lean in and go with the flow.
I'll ride to wherever our love will go.
I trust you with my heart and felt you should know.

You Make Me Smile

You make me smile.
I must admit that it has been a while since my face last had a genuine
smile.
But there it is, the smile you put on my face. Somehow you have
tapped into my happy place.
I believed it had long since gone to waste.

You make me smile.
There is just something about your charm and style.
You have me strolling down the happiness aisle.
I seem to have grins and smiles for at least a mile.
I feel special, like I'm the Queen of the Nile.

You make me smile.
You make me smile.

Time

What I need from you is time and preferential preference.
You should love me as Christ loved the church, as a point of reference.
I don't need every moment of your time as that would be insane.
I want to be a priority so I know our relationship is not in vain.

We make time for what is important to us.
If you cannot make time for me, there is nothing to discuss.
You make time for what you value, and that truth we can trust.
For a relationship with me, time given is a must.

A man makes a way, not an excuse.
I will not argue over time, so let's call it a truce.
I will not fight for your time, so please feel free to set me loose.
Your time should be given lovingly and not feel like painful abuse.

If you do not have time for me, that tells it all.
My heart aches from this reality, but this is our last call.
Without time together, our relationship is doomed to fail.
If time given doesn't change, it's just a matter of time before we both
    bail.

I Wanted

I wanted you to be my end game, but as it turns out, not so much.
I wanted you to be the last man that I would ever touch.
I wanted you to be the one with whom I'd say "I do."
I wanted you to be my forever, but that is just not you.
I wanted you to reciprocate my love, but that just didn't happen.
When it came to your love for me, in that area you were slackin'.
I wanted so much for there to be a future for you and I.
I wanted to be the last woman you loved, your ride or die.
Not getting what we want is a sad reality.
Despite us not being together, you will always have a friend in me.

Where Did the Love Go?

Where did the love go?
Honestly, I truly do not know.
I thought you were the answer to a prayer.
Initially you were a dream but became a nightmare.
How foolish of me to think my life you'd share?
Over time your actions toward me were devoid of care.
How on earth could I be so unaware?
I do believe that there was once love there.
When I check the love cupboards, now they are bare.

Where did the love go?
It seems to have slipped out the window.
Now anger and despair are in overflow.
The relationship we once shared is not salvageable.
What lies before us, I do not know.
As we divide our assets, will your greed show?
The words out of the mouth comes from what's buried below.

You betrayed my love.

The love we once shared is lost.

Liturgical

Dwell in Me

Dwell in me, Lord
Dwell in me, Lord
Dwell in me, Lord
I need you to dwell in me

He that dwelleth in the secret place of the most high,
Shall abide, shall abide, shall abide with the Lord.

Dwell in me, Lord
Dwell in me, Lord
Dwell in me, Lord
I need you to dwell in me

Through the Pain

In the midst of your pain, know that Jesus reigns.
In the midst of your pain, know that Jesus reigns.

In this life, there will be pain.
On the just and the unjust, it will rain.
When your heart is broken, you must push through. Please remember and know that God is there with you.

In the midst of your pain,
Through your pain,
Jesus reigns, Jesus reigns.

Lord, You never promised that this life would be easy.
No, that is not what your Word says.
For you said, Take up your cross, and follow me.
For my yolk is easy and my burdens are light.
If we hold fast to Your will and to Your way,
God will bring us to a brighter day.

Your pain is now a thing of the past,
And God's love will eternally last.
Through the pain, my God always reigns.
Yes, He reigns in spite of the pain.

I Will Sing and Praise

Nothing shall separate me from the love of God.
I pray when I see the pearly gates, I'll get the approval nod.

I will sing, I will sing, to the Lord in the rain.
I will praise, I will praise, the Lord through my pain.

Oh Lord, I will lift Your name on high and give You praise. When I
    think about Your goodness, my hands I will raise.

I will love and live for you for the rest of my days.
Lord, you are perfectly holy in all of Your ways.

Surrender All

Lord, I come before your throne,
acknowledging I am not my own.
I surrender all.

Here I am on bended knee,
asking you to please help me.
Hear my earnest plea.
I surrender all.

Yes, I surrender all.
Even when I fall, I still surrender all.
Even when I sin, you help me begin again.
You are my all and all,
So I'll continue to surrender all.

Here I stand, here I kneel.
Lord, please help me to be still.
Help me to submit to Your will.
I surrender all.

Unto You, oh Lord, do I lift up my soul,
For I know that only You can make me whole.
Yes, You. Only You can make me whole.

Chorus:
I surrender all.
Yes, I surrender all.
Even when I fall, I still surrender all.

Even when I sin, you help me begin again.
You are my all and all,
So I'll continue to surrender all.

Flash back

Flash back
Remember what God has brought you through.
Flash back
Recall what God has done for you.

Stand up, clap now, lift up your voice.
Come on, come on, now, let us all rejoice.
Flash back
Take a moment to flash back.

Sometimes we get too comfortable
And entitled to what God can do.
Sometimes we really don't praise Him
Like we know we really ought to.
It is often in these times,
that we need to get on track.
It is in these times, we need to flash back.

Flash back
Remember what God has brought you through.
Flash back
Recall what God has done for you.

Time to take a moment,
And recall how good God is.
Despite our sinful ways,
He is with us all our days.

Flash back, flash back
Let us stay on track.

Flash back
Remember what God has brought you through.
Flash back
Recall what God has done for you.

Sing in the Rain

In this life, a little rain must fall.
Lord, I thank you, for You will see me through it all.
Even in the times when my heart breaks.
I won't let this world my joy take.

I will sing in the rain.
I will dance through my pain.
Your name I will lift on high, and sing hallelujah,
You're worthy, You're worthy.

As I look around, at my circumstance,
I sometimes feel, I don't have a chance.
But God, but God, can do anything but fail.
His spirit whispers to my soul, "All is well."

I will sing in the rain.
I will dance through my pain
Your name I will lift on high,
And sing hallelujah,
You're worthy, You're worthy.

Despite my breaking heart, the rain, and the pain.
Through the grace of God, my strength I'll regain.
Weeping may endure for a night,
But joy comes in the morning time.

I will sing in the rain.
I will dance through my pain.
Your name I will lift on high,
And sing hallelujah,
You're worthy, You're worthy

What It's About

It's not about who I am
It's not about who I am
But it's about whose I am
About whose I am

I am a child of the Most High God.
When this life is finished, I long to receive His holy nod.
I must let my light shine in this dark world and not slack.
I must not fear, for Jesus has my back.

It's not about who I am
It's not about who I am
But it's about whose I am
About whose I am

Limitless

Limitless
Limitless
God's love is limitless

For God so loved the world He gave,
He gave His only Son.
Jesus was, and still is, the ultimate sacrifice.
So when He comes knocking at your heart,
Please let Him in and don't think twice.

Limitless
Limitless
God's love is limitless

The blood of Jesus, it covers your sin.
Daily new mercies begin again and again.
The Lord only wants. He wants the best for you.
God has your back no matter what you are going through.

Limitless
Limitless
God's love is limitless

God loves you, and He loves me too.
There is no limit to what God can do.

There is no limit to His love.
God is omnipresent from His throne above.

Limitless
Limitless
God's love is limitless

Sing

Sing, sing, sing,
Sing, sing, sing.
Let us sing unto the Lord.
Let our praises ring unto the Lord.

Sing unto the Lord.
Sing a brand new song.
Sing unto the Lord.
Praise His name all day long.

Let your praises rise
High above the skies.
Sing your song out loud.
Let our praise make God proud.

Sing, sing, sing,
Sing, sing, sing.
Let us sing unto the Lord
Let our praises ring unto the Lord.

Keep a praise on your lips
And a song in your heart.
Hold fast to the word of God
And from His spirit, never depart.

Whether you sing your song out loud,
Or meditate on it within,
Just keep your focus of praise on God
And know that with Him, you will win.

Sing, sing, sing,
Sing, sing, sing.
Let us sing unto the Lord
Let our praises ring unto the Lord.

You can conquer anything
With Jesus Christ on your side.
Humble yourself before Him,
And put aside your pride.

For God so loved the world
He gave His only begotten Son.
No matter what this world throws at you,
The final battle is already won!

You Can't Stop My Praise

Dark clouds may sometimes rise
Strong winds will sometimes blow
Even when my ship is capsized
There is one thing the world should know
This won't stop my praise
No, this can't stop my praise
No, this can't stop my praise
At times I fall down

Sometimes

Sometimes I'm cynical, satirical, right from the start.
God sees me for who I really am; He look at my heart.
He sees past my failures, and when I yield to sin.
He covers me with Jesus' blood, so I can start again.

Sometimes I lose sight of all He's done for me.
Sometimes I forget that I already have the victory.
Sometimes I get caught up and try to do things on my own.
Sometimes I may start to stray, but to God I belong.

Sometimes I forget to hold tight to God's unchanging hand.
God is in control; He has a master plan.
So when you feel down, remember you are never out.
God can always fix it, without a doubt.

Trust

Trust and believe, have faith to receive.
Trust that when you call, He will catch you when you fall.
How do you call on the Lord?
With a cry, a shout, or a beautiful musical chord?
How do you praise His name, the one whom we adore?
Hallelujah, hosanna, Sweet Rose of Sharon, or just a mumbling groan?

Dynamite

Dynamite
Dynamite
Let your praises explode
Let the praises ignite
Like dynamite
Let your spirit ignite with praise, it's all right
Let your praises explode like dynamite.

Praise Him

Praise Him, praise Him
Come on, let us praise Him, praise Him.
Praise Him, Praise Him
Come on and, praise the Lord with me.

We are all blessed, in so many ways.
So why are we so reluctant, to give God His praise?
Praise Him in the morning, when you rise and shine.
Praise Him for your meals, before you start to dine.
Praise Him for traveling grace, as you move along.
Praise Him with a shout, or even a song.

Praise Him, praise Him
Come on, let us praise Him, praise Him.
Praise Him, praise Him
Come on and, praise the Lord with me.

The holy Word of God says, in 1 Peter 2:9:
"We are a chosen people,
We are a royal priesthood,
We are a holy nation,
We are God's special possession,
We may declare, the praises of Him,
that called us out of darkness,
and in to His wonderful light."
So let us

Praise Him, praise Him
Come on, let us praise Him, praise Him.
Praise Him, praise Him
Come on and, praise the Lord with me.

The Struggle Is Real

The struggle is real, so real.
The struggle is real, so real.
The struggle, the struggle is real.

We all sin, and fall short of the glory of God.
The devil didn't make me do it,
but he showed me a great facade.
I got caught up, and fell victim to my sin.
I was in a spiritual hole and questioned if I could begin again.
The struggle is real, so real.
The struggle is real, so real.
The struggle, the struggle is real.

I could neither fix nor forgive me,
But I knew that Jesus could.
It took a while for me to take it to His throne
like I knew that I should.
His grace and mercy, it pulled me through.
There is nothing too hard for God, nothing He cannot do.

The struggle is real, so real.
The struggle is real, so real.
The struggle, the struggle is real.

When life seems, to come at you too fast.
When you are stuck in sin, or fixated on your wrongs from the past.
Remember, you have Jesus.
He is always there.

You can take all of your problems to Him.
He really does care.
Jesus looks beyond your faults, and forgives your sins.
His grace and mercy, is there for you again and again. So no matter
what, you are going through. Allow God's love, to carry you.

The struggle is real, so real.
The struggle is real, so real.
The struggle, the struggle is real.

We may fall down, repeatedly, but through the blood of Jesus Christ,
in the end, we have the victory.
No matter what trap, the devil sets for you,
He cannot take, your salvation away from you.
The struggle will be over one day, and you can rise again.
For in Jesus Christ, you have a forever friend.
So go ahead and shout praises, in God's name.
In the end, we have the victory, and shall join Him as He reigns.

We shall join Him as He reigns.
The struggle was real, but now it's over.
We shall join Him as He reigns.

I Can Do All Things

I can do all things, through Christ who strengthens me.

I can say to that mountain, Be thou removed.
I can say to the storm, I will come through.
I can say to my fear, that I will persevere
Because I
Because I can
Because I can do all

I can do all things, through Christ who strengthens me.

I can say to my problems, You will not last.
I can say to my sins, I'm forgiven and they're in my past.
I can step out on faith, knowing God will make a way.
Because I
Because I can
Because I can do all

I can do all things, through Christ who strengthens me.

For God has not given me a spirit of fear.
I must exercise my faith and wipe away any tears.
Because I
Because I can
Because I can do all

I can do all things, through Christ who strengthens me.

See

Thank you, Lord, for blessing me.
Even when I was blind and could not see.
See the error of my ways.
For sight lost for days, months, or even years.
You kept me and dried my tears.
I was blinded by sin, but You helped me see again.
Thank you, Lord, for loving me
Even when I was blind and could not see
That my actions were not aligned with Thee.

Beyond a Second Chance

Man often fixates on another man's sin.
Through the blood of Jesus Christ, we are new again.
There is no limit to God's love.
He sees past your sin from heaven above.
With God's grace, you can walk with your head held high,
Despite being within earshot of your fellow man's sigh.
I'm so thankful that God looks beyond my faults.

I Love You, Lord

I love you, Lord, and I wanted you to know that.
I'm sorry that my actions, don't always show that.
Distractions of this life, can often lead me astray.
Far from Your will, and far from Your way.

My dear Lord, I wanted You to know that
I really do, sincerely love You.
I love You, Lord.
I love You, Lord.
I love You, Lord.

I will try to let my life light shine, so that others can see.
See the grace, mercy, and blessings, You have given to me.
That it's not for any good, that I have done.
It's because of Jesus's sacrifice, God's only begotten Son.

So I wanted to let You know, that I will try to tell the world and show
    that,
I really do, sincerely love You.
I love You, Lord.
I love You, Lord.
I love You, Lord.

Nothing

Once you let Jesus, into your heart,
there is nothing, that will make Him depart
from you.
There is nothing that you can do,
to make God stop loving you.
There is nothing that you can do,
to make God stop loving you.

The love of Jesus is vast and wide,
In His presence, we shall abide.
We shall abide under the shadow of the Almighty.

We try to live according to God's Word.
But when we fail, we often try to bail, and turn away from God due
    to our sin and shame.
I challenge you to stay and bless His holy name.
There is nothing that you can do,
to make God stop loving you.

You

I'm not required to serve You,
But I long to.
Salvation is a gift of grace,
and for that, I thank You.

Your greatest gift of love
You sent to earth from heaven above.
His name is Jesus Christ,
And He made the ultimate sacrifice.
He paid His life for my sins.
So that I may live with Him
In eternity.

I'm not required to serve You,
But I long to.
Salvation is a gift of grace,
and for that, I thank You.

I will try to walk steadfast in your word,
And spread the good news to those who haven't heard.
I will try to be a light in this world today,
So that others may see the way
Unto you.

In the Midst

In the midst of Jesus, you can find joy.
In the midst of Jesus, you can find peace.
In the midst of Jesus, you can find love.
All the blessings that you find, they come from above.

Jesus, I will never, never ever, no,
I will never forget, all you have done for me.
You hung your head and died, way back in Calvary.
You sacrificed your life for me. The end battle is won because of
    Thee.

In the midst of Jesus, I have strength to withstand my mess.
In the midst of Jesus, my struggles are,
only a test.
In the midst of Jesus, I only have to call on His name.
For in the midst of Jesus, after I call on His name, nothing's ever the
    same.

Drifted Away

I drifted away from you
Even though my love was true.
You remained faithful to me,
Even when my actions did not agree,
with Your word, with Your word.

I drifted away, I drifted away,
And by my side You did stay.
I drifted away, I drifted away,
And by my side You did stay.

The world drew me in,
I didn't even recognize my sin.
I became lost in worldly ways,
From Your will I did stray.

I drifted away, I drifted away,
And by my side You did stay.
I drifted away, I drifted away,
And by my side You did stay.

Got Praise

I've got praise
I've got praise
I've got praise
This world has often weighed me down,
that my smile turned into a frown.
My mind was once filled with so much despair,
In regards to livin' my life, I no longer cared.

The hand of God, it would not let me go,
And the depth of His love, He did show.
The spirit of the Lord encouraged me
To see a doc and get the help that I need.

The word of God, yes, it spoke to me,
From those negative thoughts I did flee.

Do you ever wake up and want to lift your hand?
You've got praise
Do you ride in your car, rockin' your praise dance?
You've got praise

When you're feeling sad and down, and no one is around,
When you're feeling all alone,
Do you sing that special gospel song?
Sometimes you might cry, and then God, He wipes your eyes.
You've got praise
You've got praise
You've got praise

In Jesus

There is hope, in Jesus.
There is joy, in Jesus.
There is love, in Jesus.
There is salvation, in Jesus Christ.

The world in which we live can be a cold and brutal place.
In Jesus we can stand against whatever we must face.
In Jesus there is joy, peace, and an abundance of grace.
In Jesus we have victory at the end of our life's race.

Satisfied with Jesus

I am satisfied with Jesus. Lord, I am satisfied with You.
You provide all of my needs, and I am forever indebted to you.
There is nothing that I have done for you to love me so.
I raise my hands and lift my voice in praise just to let you know.
I am satisfied with Jesus beyond what anyone can possibly perceive.
Thank You, Jesus, for sacrificing Your life, and in You I believe.

Quarantine

At this time, we all, are going through.
I've got, a message just for you.
Do not be mean due to our circumstance.
Lift your hands and praise God with a dance.

Praise Him, in the midst of our quarantine.
Praise Him, even if you test positive for COVID-19.
Lift Him up, and praise Him in advance.
For He will, deliver you, so praise Him while you have a chance.

Praise God with a clap of your hands.
Praise Him with a song.
Praise Him with a dance. Praise Him all day long.

Your praise can be in your heart, mind, or soul.
Just praise Jesus, for He will make you whole.
Praise Him right now and every chance that you get.
Lifting His name on high is something you will not regret.

He inhabits the praises of His people,
And His love for us on this earth, there is no equal.
When the praises go up, the blessings come down,
So lift Him on up, so His joy may abound.

New Day

When I wake in the morning and the light shines in.
I'm reminded of Your mercies that are brand new again and again.
Each new day brings new hope. Because of Your love, I can cope.
Because of your love, I can cope.
When at the end of my rope, You bring me hope.

All I need to do is turn toward You.
I'm reminded of Your goodness.
I'm reminded of Your grace.
I'm reminded of the love I feel in Your sweet embrace.

Our world is a crazy, hectic place,
Lord, I long to see You face to face.
The race is not given to the swift or strong,
So follow Him even if you've been wrong.
The race is given to those who endure and finish the race.
So stick to the fight and maintain your pace.

We Are All

We are all God's children
We are all afforded God's grace and mercy given
We are all sinful in His sight
Jesus paid for our salvation in the ultimate fight
Jesus calls us to love and do what is right

Don't pass judgment on your fellow man
Try to lead by example and do the best you can

God Is

Because God is
I know that I can be
Even when in a state of misery
He puts joy deep down in my soul
For His love continues to make me whole

Because God is
When I fall victim to the enemy
Even when I believe the lies the enemy tells me
God pulls me out of that state of despair
He showers me with His love, and I know He cares

Because God is
When I lose my song
He comes to my aid and helps me along
God gives strength to my inner man
God whispers to my soul and helps me to stand

Now

Lord, I need You now
Lord, I need You now
Lord, I need You, now

Lord, I need You now
There is pain in my heart
This world can be so cruel, and I don't want to fall apart.
So I'm hastening to Your throne
For I know I'm not alone
So Lord, I need You now

Lord, I need You now
Lord, I need You now
Lord, I need You, now

Oh Lord, I need You now
I need Your Holy Spirit to comfort me
Open my spiritual eyes so I can see
Which road I should take as You lead me
So I'm casting all my cares on You, for I know that You will see me
    through
So Lord, I need You now

Lord, I need You now
Lord, I need You now
Lord, I need, You now

Power in Prayer

There is power in prayer
Power in prayer
The Lord is right there
For there is power in prayer

Sometimes we must fall on our knees
Petition the Lord with our pleas
We humbly come before Your throne
For You are God
You are God alone

There is power in prayer
Power in prayer
The Lord is right there
For there is power in prayer

Fighting Fear with Faith

I was riding with my daughter as she was driving, and God began to
   whisper to me.
I stayed quiet, and I listened to the Holy Spirit intensely.
A message was being ministered to me.

I heard that still, small voice from within.
The one that draws your spiritual ear to Him. The one that makes
   you feel the warmth of His presence and love.
The one that makes you harken unto it because you know it's sent
   from above.

"We must fight fear with faith!" resonated in my soul.
"We must do this if we want to be whole."
Hmmm, okay, Lord, so what does that mean?
On Christ we must depend. On Him we must lean.

All right, Lord, I believe that is what I already do.
The Lord replied, "Not completely, so let Me break it down for you.
When you worry and feel in despair,
I already told you, on Me you can cast your cares.
My yoke is easy, and My burdens are light.
When you trust in Me completely, please know that everything will
   be all right.

"Come to My altar and leave your burdens there.
Trust that I know what you are going through. Trust that I am fully
   aware.

I will address it in My time alone.
As I work, I want you to hang out in the praise zone."

Yes, Lord, I will exercise my faith. I will do my best.
I will dwell in Your Spirit, for in You I will find rest.
God is attracted to our praise in the midst of our problems.
So let us praise Him while we are going through and trust in Him to
solve them.

Faith is the substance of things hoped for, the evidence of things not
seen.
After submitting problems to the Lord, we cannot let fear in between.
Daily we must "fight fear with faith!" And know that faith will always
win.
We must trust the abundance of God's love and know that He will
always be there again and again.

Jesus

On the mighty, matchless name of Jesus
You can always call
Trust that Jesus
He will catch you when you fall

You don't have to be perfect
You are always worth it
God is always there
To provide His loving care

You will slip and fall
But on the shoulders of Jesus, you can stand tall
His love will never fail
For in Him, all is well
He will give you perfect peace and joy
It doesn't matter if you are a girl or boy
It doesn't matter how old you are
It doesn't matter if you are poor or a rich and famous star

Once you invite Jesus into your heart,
Life won't be perfect, but His grace is a good start
Bask in His love
One day you will join Him in heaven above

On the mighty, matchless name of Jesus
You can always call
Trust that Jesus
He will catch you when you fall

Glad

I'm so glad that man didn't make me.
For man can only love what they see.
God sees the creation He called me to be.
He sees the challenges I face and the victory.

Poor God

Poor God, we are a people who can't be pleased.
But God is so good He still hears our pleas.
People with curly hair want it straight.
People with straight hair, they hate.
People who are short want to be tall.
Tall people don't want to linger above all.
We must learn to be thankful in whatever state we are in.
We must thank God for the forgiveness of our sin.

Two Times

There are only two times to praise the Lord.
When you feel like it and when you don't.
So give Him the praise, for He is who we adore.
Do not let your praise become a chore.
It should be fun as we worship the Son.

When you don't want to praise, that is the best time to raise,
Raise your hands, and do a praise dance.
It is hard to stay down when Jesus comes around.
He will fill you with joy that this world cannot destroy.
Do not believe the lies the enemy will deploy.

There are only two times to praise the Lord.
When you feel like it and when you don't.

About the Author

Dr. Tiffanie Tate Moore is a first-time author from Compton, California. She is a graduate of UC Santa Barbara where she earned a bachelor of science degree in cellular and developmental biology, with a Black studies minor. After earning her medical doctorate degree from Meharry Medical College and completing her OBGYN Internship at Naval Medical Center San Diego, she went on to serve as a general medical officer for the Sea Bees. She served during Operation Enduring Freedom, during the Global War on Terrorism. Dr. Moore completed her obstetrics and gynecology residency at Vanderbilt University Medical Center in Nashville, Tennessee, and practiced for twenty years before sustaining a hand injury that led to her medical retirement. She began writing poems as an outlet for her emotions.

Dr. Tate Moore maintains her board-certified status with the American Board of Obstetrics and Gynecology and speaks on women's health issues. She is an ordained wedding official with the Universal Life Church and a loving mother of two young adults. She stays active in her community by serving her church as a trustee, singing with her church choir, and being active in the graduate chapter of her sorority. The shared life experiences of her and her friends have overflowed into *FloweTry*.